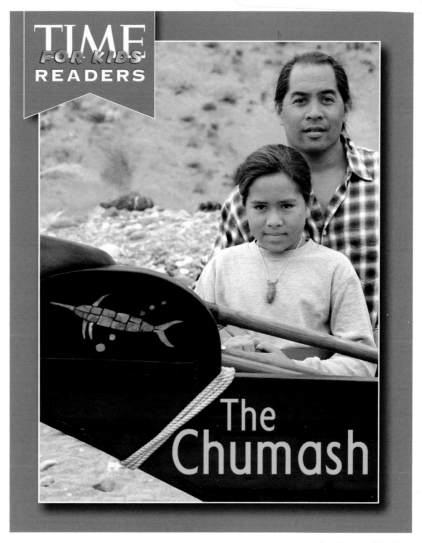

# The Chumash

**by Renee Skelton**

Harcourt
SCHOOL PUBLISHERS

Orlando   Austin   New York   San Diego   Toronto   London

Visit *The Learning Site!*
**www.harcourtschool.com**

# The Chumash

Today the Santa Barbara Channel is a busy sea highway. But hundreds of years ago, the channel— a narrow, deep waterway between two areas of land— was used only by the Chumash (CHOO•mash), an American Indian tribe.

HOME OF THE CHUMASH TRIBE

OREGON

NEVADA

CALIFORNIA

Santa Barbara Channel

•San Luis Obispo

•Santa Ynez

•Malibu

Channel Islands

PACIFIC OCEAN

MEXICO

Many Chumash lived on the coast in the southern part of California—from what is now Malibu to San Luis Obispo—and on the Channel Islands.

The Chumash who lived on the mainland of California often crossed the channel by boat to reach the Channel Islands. They braved rough waters. Sometimes they had to find their way to the islands through thick fog.

Today the Chumash cross the Santa Barbara Channel in a canoe, just as their ancestors (AN•ses•terz) did in the past. An ancestor is a member of your family who lived long ago.

## Expert Canoe Builders

The Chumash made canoes, called *tomols* (TOH•mohlz), from logs from redwood trees. One large plank formed the bottom of the canoe. Several other planks formed the sides. Rope made from plant fibers was slipped through holes in the planks to hold them together.

The Chumash also used tar to seal cracks. This kept out most of the water. Young boys often went along on ocean trips. They helped scoop water out of the boat to keep it afloat.

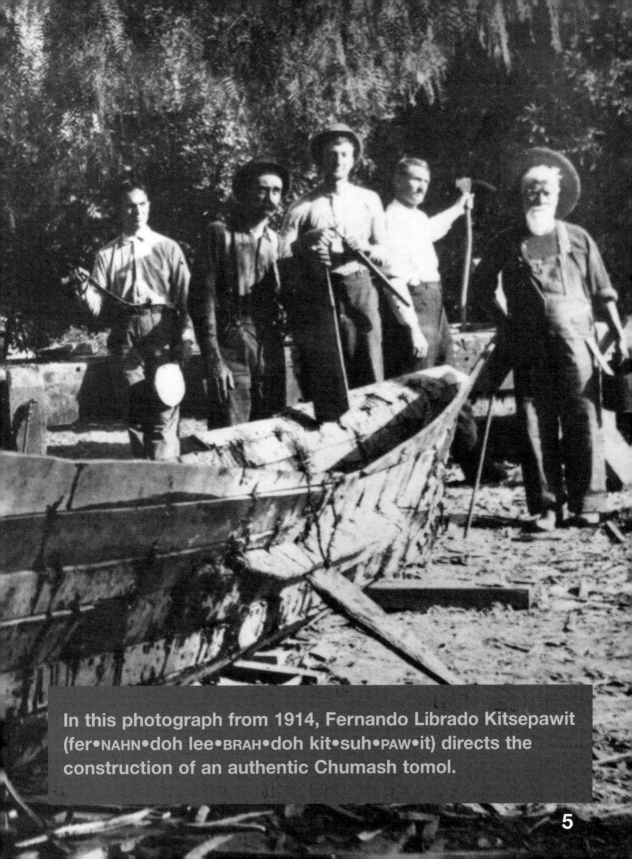

In this photograph from 1914, Fernando Librado Kitsepawit (fer•NAHN•doh lee•BRAH•doh kit•suh•PAW•it) directs the construction of an authentic Chumash tomol.

## Money from the Sea

The Chumash made shell money from olivella, or purple olive, snails. They strung these shells on plant fibers to make strands like necklaces. Long strands of shells were worth more than short ones. Beads made from the small, thick part of the shell were worth more than those made from other parts.

The Chumash who lived on the Channel Islands used the shell money to trade with mainland Chumash. They traded for rabbit skins, deer hides and antlers, and plants.

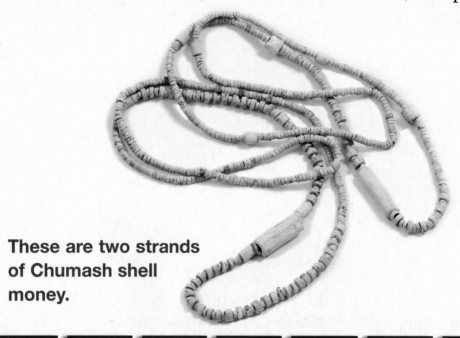

**These are two strands of Chumash shell money.**

## Chumash Crafts

The Chumash were well known for their beautiful baskets. Chumash baskets have unique designs. Many have a border about 1 inch wide around the edge. Some have black bars that run up and down on the basket sides. Others have zigzag lines. The Chumash used the baskets to carry plants and water, store shell money, cook, and even carry babies.

Today some people in California are preserving the old ways of basket weaving.

**This is a shallow Chumash basket.**

## Chumash Food

The Chumash depended on the Pacific Ocean for food. Skilled fishers caught fish and other sea animals with nets or spears. They also gathered clams and mussels. The mainland Chumash used bows and arrows to hunt animals, such as deer.

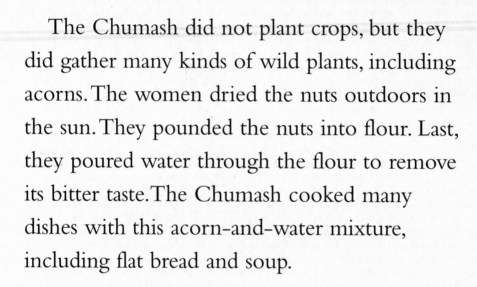

The Chumash did not plant crops, but they did gather many kinds of wild plants, including acorns. The women dried the nuts outdoors in the sun. They pounded the nuts into flour. Last, they poured water through the flour to remove its bitter taste. The Chumash cooked many dishes with this acorn-and-water mixture, including flat bread and soup.

These tools were used by the Chumash to catch large fish and sea mammals.

The Chumash used these tools to grind acorns into flour.

# A Chumash Village

The Chumash lived in hundreds of settlements. The largest Chumash settlements were on the coast near the Santa Barbara Channel. They were usually built near a lake or stream, so the tribe would have fresh water nearby.

The Chumash lived in houses called *aps* (AHPS), which were shaped like upside-down bowls. To build an ap, Chumash men stuck willow poles into the ground in a circle. They bent the poles toward the center. Then they tied them together to make the bowl shape. They tied smaller branches cross-wise between the willow poles. Finally they placed rushes, or long, hollow plants, over the frame.

**A Chumash village**

They left a hole in the top of the ap to let out the smoke from the cooking fire. When it rained, they covered the hole with a woven rush mat. Usually five to seven people would live in one ap. They slept on platform beds. Below the beds, they stored personal items, such as clothing, tools, and baskets.

# Daily Life

A person's position in the Chumash community was determined by his or her job. Most workers were on the bottom level. People who made tools, built boats, and wove baskets had a higher position. Priests and healers had very high positions. Chiefs were usually the wealthiest and most powerful people. Both women and men could be priests, healers, and chiefs.

The Chumash also liked to have fun and played games such as the hoop and pole game. In this game, boys pushed a small hoop, 4 or 5 inches wide. As the hoop rolled, players on either side of it tried to throw 6-foot-long spears through it. One point was given for each time the spear went through the hoop. Two or more people played until someone had 12 points and won the game.

**Recently, some people have returned to the art of building Chumash tomols and have used them to cross the Santa Barbara Channel.**

## The Chumash at Spanish Missions

When Spain first explored the coast of California in the mid-1500s, there were thousands of Chumash people living there and on the Channel Islands.

In the late 1700s the Spanish began to set up missions in California, which was then part of Mexico. A mission was a Spanish settlement that was run by priests. The Chumash who lived at a mission worked on the mission's farm and took care of its cattle. They had to become Christians, learn the Spanish language, and dress and live like the Spanish.

It became difficult for the Chumash to survive without accepting some Spanish ways of life. However, many continued to secretly practice their traditional religion and Chumash ways of life.

In 1821 Mexico became independent of Spain. Mexico promised to give back to the Chumash some of their lands. Instead, the government sold almost all of the mission lands to settlers. By the late 1800s, many Chumash communities were gone.

This sketch of the Mission of San Buenaventura was made by Henry Miller in 1856. The Chumash helped build the mission.

## The Chumash Today

The Chumash passed their history down with stories told by parents to children. Many of the stories are still alive in the hearts and minds of the Chumash.

The Chumash still live in southern California. Some families live in Santa Ynez, California, on the Santa Ynez Reservation, which was created in 1902. Others live in towns and cities along California's coast.

Today the Chumash want to keep their heritage alive. That way, people in the future will know about them and their contributions to California.